D1370682

All photographs by
Giulio Veggi except the following:

Carlo Borienghi / Sea & See Italia:
58-59, 70-71
Sea & See Italia:
61
David Messent / APA Photo Agency:
62-63
Dennis Lane / APA Photo Agency:
64, 68
Bill Mc Causland / APA Photo Agency:
66
J. Murphy / APL Sea & See Italia:
69
John Heaton / APA Photo Agency:
72-73

© 1991 White Star
Via C. Sassone, 24, Vercelli, Italy.

All rights reserved. Reproduction of the whole or any part of the
contents, without written permission, is prohibited.

Printed and bound in Singapore.

First published in English in 1991 by
Tiger Books International PLC, London

This 1991 edition published by
Crescent Books, distributed by
Outlet Book Company, Inc.
A Random House Company
225 Park Avenue South
New York
New York 10003

ISBN 0-517-05879-0
87654321

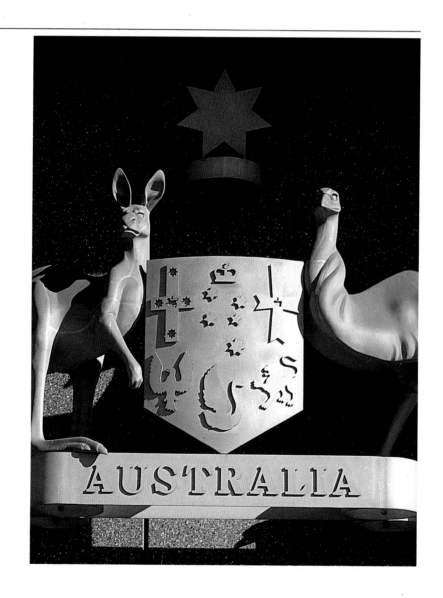

INSIDE
SYDNEY

TEXT
FABIO BOURBON

DESIGN
PATRIZIA BALOCCO

PHOTOGRAPHS
GIULIO VEGGI

CRESCENT BOOKS
New York

2-3 Sydney-siders are very proud of the futuristic and elegantly complex structure of the Opera House.

4 The city coat of arms stands out clearly on the facade of the Supreme Court Building.

6 Sydney Cove, the small inlet where Governor Arthur Phillip disembarked with his settlers, is now called Circular Quay, dominated by the modern high-rise buildings of the commercial district.

7 In the foreground are the northern suburbs and the gigantic Harbour Bridge; in the centre are the Rocks, the skyscrapers of the city and, on the left, the Opera House.

Every city has its own personality which it fosters: Sydney's is brash, lively, successful, but a bit uncouth. It has a simple lay-out: the "city" – the business and cultural district – is in the middle; the port and the industrial area stretch along the bay while, around them, the immense suburbs stretch out for many square miles. The ingredients for a rather special alchemy are all there and range from Sydney's enormous size to the fact that it is the cradle of modern Australia, which is lucky enough to have having a charming climate and be surrounded by a splendid landscape.

Considered by many to be the uncontested capital of the South Pacific, Sydney is situated on the banks of an inlet called Port Jackson, one of the safest and most beautiful gulfs in the world. It was created by the sinking of the coastline, as a result of which the sea entered far inland, occupying the lower valley of the Parramatta River. The centre of the city is on the southern shore, around the oldest settlement, but the city has developed inland as far as the Blue Mountains, occupying the miniscule peninsulas which stud the coast. Sydney is roughly divided into its northern and southern parts by the Harbour Bridge. The North Shore consists basically of residential suburbs and light industry.

The centre of the economic and commercial life is the port. This is the best equipped and busiest in the whole of Australia and port of call for the regular navigation lines which ply the Pacific and Indian Oceans. The industrial zone has developed towards the south and has progressively occupied all the available space as far as Botany Bay where we find the international airport, called Kingsford Smith.

Sydney is a true metropolis containing about a quarter of the national population: anyone who wanted to cross it on foot would be letting himself in for an adventure, given that the urban conglomerate extends for a distance of around 60 miles from north to south. It is difficult to believe that all this is the result of barely two centuries of settlement, yet, now that the difficult years of pioneering, uncontrolled immigration and defensive and racist provincialism are relegated to the history books, modern-day Australia is a relaxed and satisfied country whose cosmopolitan heart, Sydney, pulsates with life.

In the past, the outlook was far from rosy. For centuries Australia was a mythical place in the imaginations of Europeans who had visions of gold, power and glory, but, despite innumerable attempts, the geologically oldest continent with all its mystery and immense riches, was the last to be discovered. As long ago as the Renaissance there were fantasies about an unknown land which was thought to occupy the largest part of the southern hemisphere. Before that, Chinese and Arab navigators had reached Australia only to leave again immediately. Much later, the Portuguese and Dutch did the same. Disappointed not to find fabulous profits and frightened by the inhospitable appearance of boundless scrublands and their wild inhabitants, they were convinced they had missed their target.

Although it might seem incredible, all those intrepid navigators had missed the fertile eastern coast by just a few miles and it was not until Captain Cook cast anchor in the luxuriant Botany

8 The figure of the mythical "bushman", the tough and adventurous frontiersman is now only a legend. Today, the modern Sydney-sider is elegant, dynamic and not at all keen to do without the comforts of a technologically advanced civilization.

Bay in April 1770, that the dream which the West had fondly toyed with since the times of Marco Polo came true.

Cook realized that he had touched an unknown part of the "new continent" and his intuition gave him an idea of its outline and its immense potential. Moving further north, he sighted and named Port Jackson, the large bay of Sydney, and a few days later he gave a name to the country, i.e. to the most beautiful and fertile part of Australia, New South Wales, taking possession of it in the name of George III, King of England. Imagination had finally become reality.

Eighteen years later, Governor Arthur Phillip arrived in these waters at the head of 1,360 colonists (736 of whom were convicts), and landed at Sydney Cove in the small inlet where the Opera House now stands.

The first colony of deportees, destined to receive the undesirable elements of the Motherland, had a hard start, characterized by difficulties, cruelty and isolation. Sydney, which was named after the Secretary of State for colonial affairs, was originally nothing more than a large and chaotic camp, but the tents were soon replaced by cabins made of wood and bricks. Phillip attempted to impose an orderly and regular plan on the growing city but without success. Many of the restless inhabitants could not stand discipline and obedience to the law. The system of dirt-tracks and short-cuts which was created in the town in the course of the years, is still recognisable in the labyrinth of streets which, even today, characterizes the layout of the city.

Despite the fact that the government encouraged the

immigration of free colonists, Sydney, partly because of its bad reputation, grew very slowly up to 1850, when the discovery and exploitation of gold and the developments in cattle-raising caused a rapid increase. Deportations to the penal colonies stopped in 1868 and in that period Sydney already had a population of 120,000, which, thanks to the sharp improvement in the standard of life and the increasing economic well-being, increased rapidly after the Federation in 1901. In a little less than 200 years, the capital of New South Wales has been radically transformed, from that terrible "hell on earth" for criminals and desperadoes in search of fortune, to a futuristic metropolis with over three and a half million inhabitants.

10 This statue of Queen Victoria stands in Queen's Square, a reminder of Australia's history as part of the British Empire.

11 A monumental fountain in Hyde Park, the green lung of the city.

12-13 The business district seen from Darling Harbour Monorail Station. The electric monorail system is approximately two and a half miles long and connects the city with the Darling Harbour complex.

14 An unusual view of the city's skyscrapers, dominated by the slender profile of Sydney Tower.

15 A strip of blue sky appears fleetingly between the steep glass and concrete canyons of the commercial district.

16 The historical buildings of Circular Quay West stand out in contrast against the rigid geometric lines of the skyscrapers. In the foreground is the Dutch Gable House, built in 1883.

17 The Sydney Opera House, with its white "sails" or "shells", was partly financed by the proceeds from a public lottery. It was designed in 1957 and work started in 1959. The government estimated that it would be completed in six years at a cost of 7 million dollars. In fact, after 14 years of work, more than 102 million dollars had been spent.

18 Sydney is home to more than 60% of the population of New South Wales as well as the majority of the state's industrial, commercial and banking activities. However, despite its rapid growth, it remains a city with an undeniable charm.

19 The first light of dawn imparts a warm golden glow to the skyscrapers of Sydney Cove.

20-21 Situated on the southern promontory of the port, the suburb of Watson's Bay is tranquil and elegant.

The biggest and oldest Australian city is also the one which has the best geographical position. Spread out around the bluish-green waters of the harbour, today it is one of the most beautiful cities in the world. Only San Francisco can compete with the incomparable sight of Sydney Harbour where, as well as the vast main waterway, there are numerous creeks and bays which contribute to the really spectacular nature of this unusual urban panorama.

In Sydney, the beach is really only two steps away and the entire city lives and prospers, having evolved a very particular conception of duty and free time. In fact, quite a few Sydney-siders (as the inhabitants call themselves), go to work by ferry. During the week, the ferries which connect the centre to those suburbs which are accessible by water, unload a mass of clerks and civil servants in jackets and ties every morning and take them back to the comfort of their suburban houses in the evening. But, at lunch-time, after five o'clock and at weekends, they all follow the irresistible call of the waves of the Pacific Ocean: sun, sand and surf. The people of Sydney know how to enjoy themselves and their passion for boundless spaces and the open air will never cease to amaze visitors. To give you an idea: there are more than 5,000 yachts, motor-boats and other pleasure craft registered with the port authorities; during every sunny summer weekend the great bay becomes a crowded kaleidoscope of colours as boats of all types cruise around in incredible confusion.

There are regattas in the harbour in every season but the most famous is, without doubt, the spectacular "Sydney-Hobart" which attracts competitors from all over the world. From 1945 to date, the 680-mile race begins every year on 26th December at 11 o'clock precisely.

Despite the decidedly intense traffic, it is still possible to fish in the waters of the bay and quite a few people have experienced the emotion of pulling aboard a big catch. Lovers of suntans have no reason to be envious of the Californians, and quite rightly so: the golden-white sands of this corner of the earth are ideal for relaxation and sun-bathing. Bondi Beach is certainly the most famous Sydney beach, but there are another 30 all within a range of 12 miles from the city. Those around the port have calmer waters and, because there are also parks and play-areas close to them, they are particularly frequented by families with small children. On the other hand, the numerous beaches on the Pacific, with its huge waves, are the logical destination of hundreds of surfers who challenge each other with reckless daring.

Teams of volunteer lifesavers constantly keep an eye on the safety of the swimmers. These athletes are organized in clubs and are specialized in all the nautical sports which have anything to do with sea rescue. They use large boats known as "surfboats", which require particularly strong oarsmen to move them through the highest waves.

For many years, "surf carnivals" have been occasions for the various clubs to compete with each other: swimming competitions, relay races and boat races take place in rapid succession from November to the end of March, bringing together tens of thousands of spectators and competitors.

22-23 Every day, the giant chess-boards in Hyde Park attract enthusiastic players and spectators of all ages.

24 Hyde Park, the Domain and the Royal Botanic Gardens form a vast green area on the eastern side of the city and are perfect for walking and for relaxation.

25 In Sydney's well-groomed public gardens it is not unusual to come across groups of schoolchildren having lessons in the open-air: no scholastic text can beat the charm of direct contact with Australia's luxuriant flora.

26 Paddington flea market is the ideal place to get an excellent bargain and at the same time admire a large number of "street artists" engaged in their impromptu shows.

27 The district of Paddington, "Paddo" to the majority of the inhabitants, is a typical example of those inner suburbs which were progressively inhabited by the first bourgeoisie towards the end of the 19th century, then by workers of Anglo-Saxon origin and other immigrants of European origin.

28-29 A typical band performing in the "Hero of Waterloo", the oldest bar in Australia, which began serving its excellent beer in the far-off days of 1809.

30 top Thousands of Chinese immigrants have sought their fortunes in Australia and it will come as no surprise to learn that Sydney has its Chinatown. Dixon Street is justly proud of its oriental style.

30 bottom Darlinghurst Road is the liveliest and most bohemian street in the city.

As one would imagine, there is an awful lot to be seen in Sydney. An innovative spirit and conservative tendencies have meant that alongside ultra-modern constructions in the city there are sunny, tree-lined squares and narrow, cobbled streets dating from last century.

Once abandoned, and now the object of a thorough restoration plan, the older quarters of Sydney are experiencing a glorious period of revival. The heart of the city is spread out on the slopes around Sydney Cove and the immediate surroundings. Despite the fact that in the years since the Second World War, the city skyline has progressively taken on an appearance similar to all western metropolises, with concrete, glass and steel towers, at a lower level, a large part of the city's colonial heritage has remained intact.

Solid sandstone arches, pretty Victorian porticoes, warehouses, shops and high-class houses: the buildings which have seen Australia change from a penal colony to become a free and rich nation have finally rediscovered their second youth. The old Parliament House, St. James' Church and Hyde Park Prison Barracks all date from the first decades of the 19th Century. The last two monuments are the work of the convict Francis Greenway, who, sent to Sydney for forgery, became the principle architect of the young colony. His sober and elegant style was adopted as a model by his successors and is still admired today.

"The Rocks", the point at which the pioneers of the First Fleet built their houses, is the oldest residential area in the continent, the birthplace of Australia (the European one, that is). The

31 top Argyle Street is very different from
Darlinghurst Road in terms of tastes and style,
with its picturesque rows of well-kept houses
dating from last century.

31 bottom An uninterrupted row of shops,
offices and restaurants makes Oxford Street one of
the busiest arteries in the eastern part of the city.

criminals are long gone and now the customs sheds and
warehouses contain art galleries and rather chic restaurants.
It hardly seems possible that only 150 years ago, rum
smugglers and soldiers of the regular army fought each other
with swords and muskets on the flagstones of Argyle Square or
in the "Cut", a famous steep stairway which climbs up the hill.
Every day, they show documentaries in the Rocks Visitors'
Centre which illustrate the history of the place from the times of
Governor Phillip to the day before yesterday: here, for example,
one can discover that the oldest building in Sydney is Cadman's
Cottage, built in 1813 and now a well-frequented destination for
historical and scholarly pilgrims. Or else you will discover that
the city is dotted with a number of neo-Gothic cathedrals and
churches: the most interesting are the Garrison Church in Argyle
Place and the Anglican St. Andrew's Cathedral which is situated
near the town hall. The magnificent Catholic Cathedral of St.
Mary's is one of the largest in the world.
The access roads to the Harbour Bridge divide the Rocks area in
two and, in the western part, the social character changes
noticeably. There are numerous quiet public gardens and the
refined Georgian houses of the small local nobility. A completely
different air can be breathed in the central Martin Place, a
popular pedestrian plaza where city-workers and tourists mix to
have a quick chat while having a midday snack. Here the
architectural styles of Sydney are clearly illustrated in the
contrast between the Post Office Tower, in pure Victorian style,
and the modern stainless steel sculpture erected in the centre of
the Plaza in 1979.

32 top The neo-Gothic Catholic cathedral of St. Mary's dates from 1868 and is still one of the largest in the world.

32 bottom Macquarie Place, one of the most characteristic spots in the city, is packed with office workers at lunch-time on weekdays and almost deserted at weekends. The obelisk was erected by Francis Greenway to mark the starting point of all the roads in the continent.

The city lives completely and intimately with water, and the sea is never really far away. Sydney is the most important port in Australia with its huge warehouses, wharves and population of sailors from all over the world who meet in the dockside bars. In the last 30 years, however, the city has done a lot to try to improve its image.

Sydney Opera House is the symbol of this artistic leap ahead: a challenge to the cultural isolationism from which the whole of Australia has suffered since the "frontier" period. This imposing building with its unfurled, white, tile-covered sails and its smoked glass windows, rises up on the tip of Bennelong Point and is one of the most innovative constructions of the 20th century. Designed in 1957 by the Danish architect Jörn Utzon, it was completed 16 years later at a cost of A$102 million and inaugurated on the 20th October 1973 by Queen Elizabeth II. With its original design, the result of the engineering problems created by its ten shell-shaped sections of roof, the Opera House contains concert halls, a cinema, an exhibition centre and two restaurants. The statistical data are impressive; the roofs reach a height of 214 feet, are covered with a million Swedish ceramic tiles and are held up by 210 miles of iron cable.

All the events in the Opera House are advertised monthly at all the internal offices and in the tourist agencies of the city. Organized visits to the vast complex are held daily, and, almost every evening, operas, ballet, concerts of classical music, jazz and pop are put on. It should not be forgotten that Australia boasts artists of international renown such as the soprano

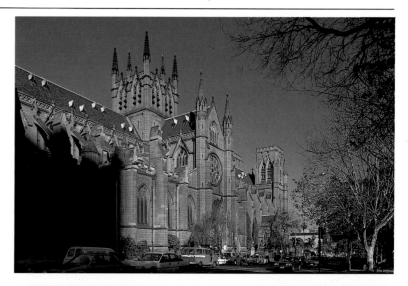

33 Queen Victoria Building, erected between 1893 and 1898, was designed by George McRae in a curious neo-Romanesque style. After having been abandoned for years, this monument of the Victorian age was reopened in 1986 after a long restoration had transformed it into a lively and elegant shopping mall. It is now known as the QVB.

Joan Sutherland; the country also has a very active rock music circuit. Even though the two principle theatres can seat several thousand spectators, its always better to book a seat in advance. In the large square in front of the Opera House, there are occasional exhibitions of popular dancing put on by the various ethnic groups in the city or more simply impromptu shows given by the city's numerous street artists.

Fifty years in time and 500 yards away from the Opera House is the equally spectacular Sydney Harbour Bridge, under whose single span large container ships and ocean liners can pass with ease. When it was built in 1932, the bridge was considered one of the technological wonders of the world. With a span of 1638 feet and eight lanes wide, it represents the principle road link between the commercial part of the city and the densely populated residential areas on the North Shore. The bridge took nine years to build and can be crossed by train, car, bus, bicycle or on foot. The 1,000-foot high Sydney Tower, with its two revolving restaurants and two observation platforms, completes the city's trio of architectural masterpieces.

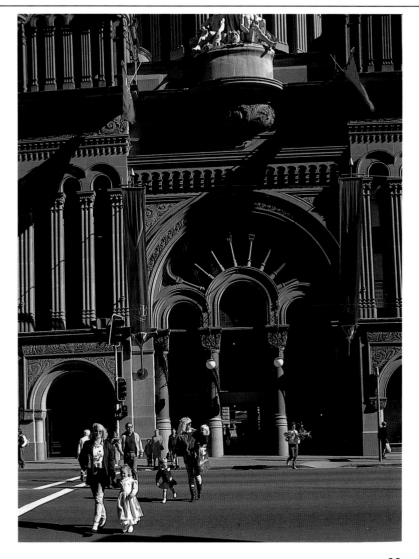

34 The little houses ot Watson's Bay cling to the slopes of the promontory which separates the placid waters of Port Jackson from the open sea.

35 Aerial view of Rushcutter's Bay with its well-organized moorings for hundreds of yachts. The nautical registers of the Sydney Port Authorities contain the details of over 5,000 vessels but the number is constantly increasing.

36-37 *A splendid view of Sydney Harbour Bridge and the elegant white shells of the Opera House.*

38-39 *One hundred and forty years after its foundation, Manly continues to be one of Sydney's most famous suburbs. In this it is enhanced by the beauty of the twin inlets of Mosman Bay and Shell Cove.*

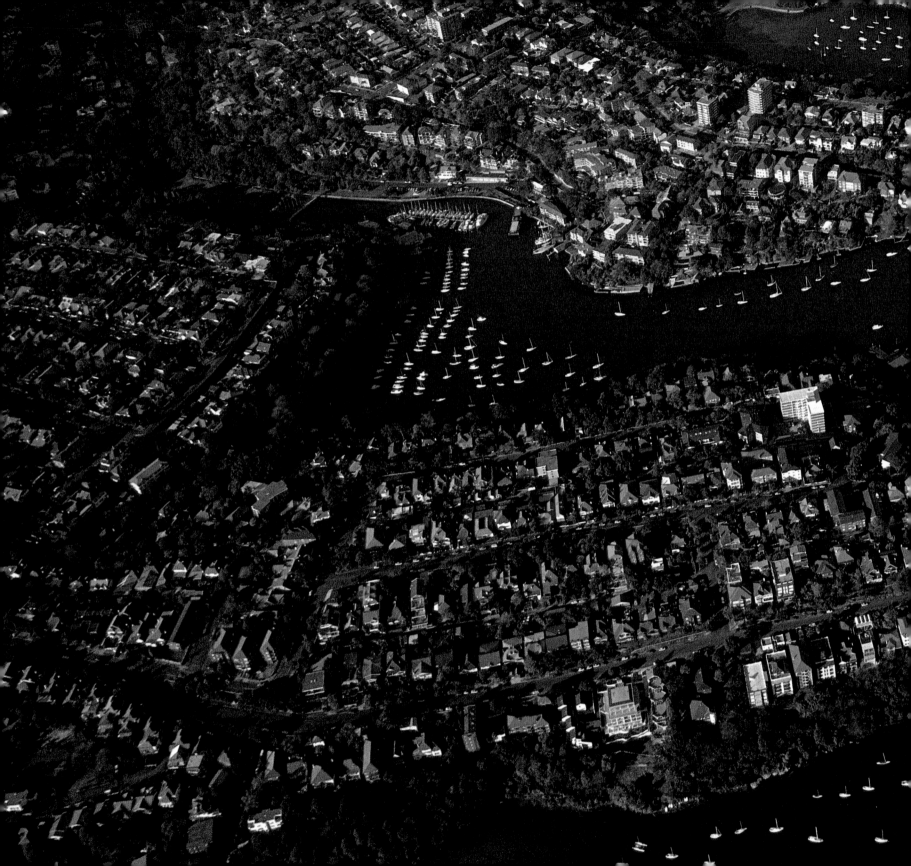

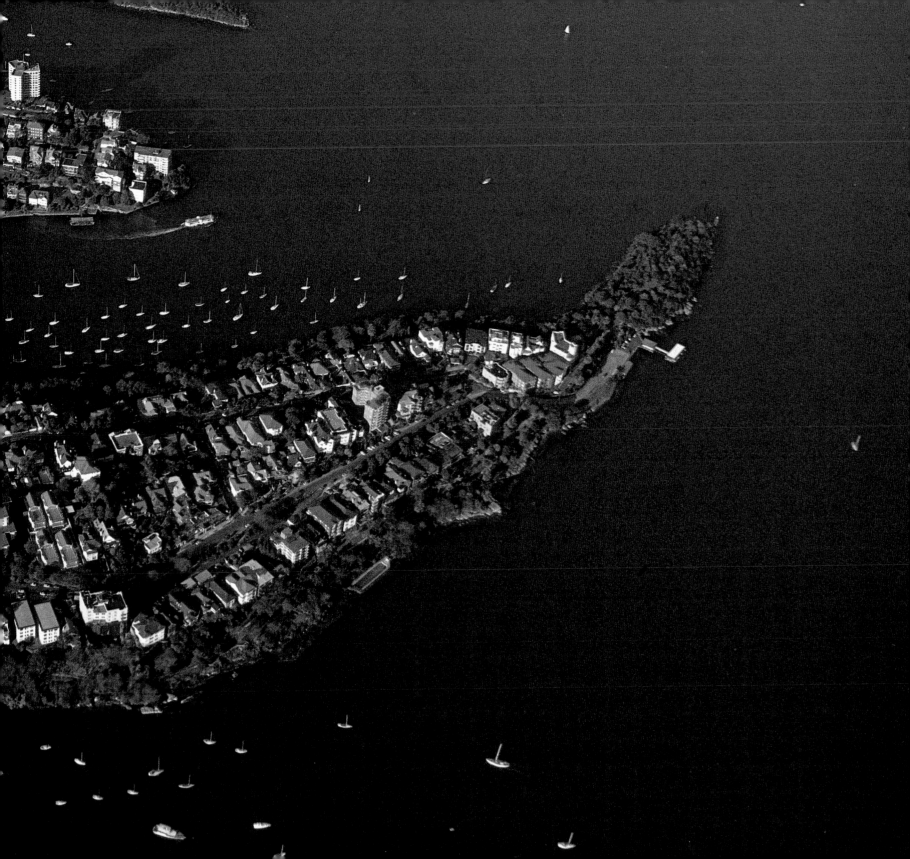

40 The obvious architectural contrasts of the city are symbolic of a metropolis whose population has grown from 200,000 to 3,500,000 in little more than a century.

41 The austere neo-Gothic lines of St. Andrew's Cathedral appear well matched to the slender outlines of the surrounding skyscrapers. The building was begun in 1819 but completed between 1837 and 1868 and is the oldest cathedral in the continent.

42 The commercial port of Sydney is one of the largest and best equipped of the southern hemisphere and every year many thousand cargo ships, belonging to merchant fleets from all parts of the world, berth here.

43 Circular Quay is the mooring place for the numerous passenger ferries which transport people between the heart of the city and the outlying suburbs.

44 Sydney Tower is 1,000 feet high and is the highest building south of the Equator. It was finished in 1981 and rises from the commercial complex called Centrepoint. The summit can be reached by means of high-speed elevators and it contains two rotating restaurants, offices, observation platforms and telecommunications equipment.

45 The Archibald Memorial Fountain in Hyde Park is a popular meeting place.

46 The famous Waterfront Restaurant in the historical Rocks area is not only renowned for its excellent cuisine but also because of its resemblance to a three-masted sailing ship, which makes it one of the most bizarre sites in the entire Pacific area.

I f you decide to take a break from sightseeing, all you have to do is walk along George Street in which there are a large number of restaurants, cafés and sandwich-bars; if you like authentic places, the nearby "Argyle Tavern" is a well-known buffet furnished with antiques. With the arrival of immigrants from all parts of the world, Australia discovered that it had a vocation for good cuisine. All possible and imaginable national cuisines are present, from Italian to Lebanese, but the great speciality of the city is sea food: all kinds of fish and shellfish with a special mention for the oysters. The most popular restaurants in Sydney are out of town, in splendid settings which add charm to the already excellent food; while we are on this subject, if you really want something "special", cross the eastern suburbs until you get to the southern promontory of the port and Watson's Bay. As well as some exceptional bars, here one can find Doyle's Sea Food Restaurant, the most famous fish restaurant in the city, and naturally, the country. It has been managed by the same family for more than a century and it has now become an institution, with a matchless menu.

This is a suitable occasion to visit the surroundings of Harbour City. The suburbs of Sydney contain a lot of pleasant surprises, like Vancluse House, an example of 20th-century elegance in the eastern suburbs.

A little further inshore, Paddington or "Paddo", as it is familiarly called, is the quarter in which many writers, artists and actors seek refuge. It is densely inhabited and characterized by multicoloured terraced houses, their walls covered with climbing plants, and a large number of shops selling curios and

47 top "Paddy's" is the largest and most popular market in Sydney and here one can find everything from food to craft objects and from books to the most splendid examples of Australian flora.

47 bottom The integration of the Aborigines in modern Australian society has not been without controversy.

48-49 An unusual Sunday scene in George Street on the corner with Argyle Street. The building in the foreground on the right is the Rocks Police Station, built in 1882.

bric à brac, as well as art galleries, bistros and bars.
The affectionate nickname of "Paddington Lace" refers to the laceworks of wrought iron which decorated the balconies of the local dwellings during the last years of the 19th century. Thanks to recent restorations, the "laces" of Paddington have once more come into prominence and many houses are quite rightly proud of their intricate ornaments.
Completely different but no less interesting is Manly, which is half-an-hour's ferry-ride from the Opera House. The suburb which looks onto the Ocean, its main attractions are its twin beaches. While one of them, which is well protected, is dedicated to the amusement of young children, the other, the famous and lively Pacific Beach, is a catwalk for shining muscles and suntanned beauties. Between the two half-moons of white sand there is the straight line of the "main street," a pedestrian zone which boasts an impressive series of cafés, snack bars, fruit shops and boutiques.
To go back to the main part of Sydney, do not hesitate to board one of the blue and white ferries, and enjoy the splendours of the city seen from the sea. Calm waters, miles of beaches and curving bays stretch out all around you. You can take your pick from the numerous guided tours and "coffee cruises" which sail across the port.

50 Young lawyers near the Supreme Court Building: the gown and the wig remind us that in Australia, as in other countries of Anglo-Saxon origin, there is a great love for tradition.

50

51 The reinforced concrete "sails" of the Opera House merge with the golden outline of Sydney Tower. The tiles which cover the complex are self-cleaning and become perfectly white again after every shower of rain.

52 top The suburb of Manly is rightly appreciated for its numerous ethnic restaurants which represent many of the culinary traditions of the world.

52 bottom "Doyle's on the Beach" at Watson's Bay is one of the most famous restaurants in Sydney: the tables are on the beach, the view of the Harbour is grand and the fish cooked in the style of "fish and chips" is delicious.

53 Named after the street in Rome, the Corso is the best known commercial artery in Manly. A multicolored bustling pedestrian zone, it boasts an incredible number of bars, snack bars, bazaars and boutiques in its relatively short length.

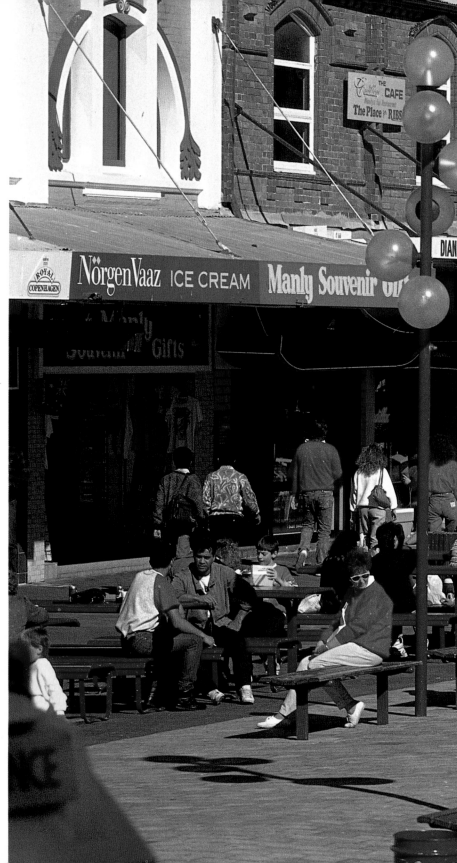

54 Fishing in the waters of Bondi is one of the
favourite pastimes of Sydney-siders.

55 With its perfect half-moon of white sand,
Bondi Beach is the most frequented and loved of
the more than 30 beaches in the area around
Sydney and is perhaps the most famous in
Australia.

56 From the top of the precipitous cliff at Commodore Heights in the Ku-Ring-gai Chase National Park, one can enjoy a magnificent panorama of Broken Bay, delineated on the right by the Barrenjoey peninsula, extreme northern offshoot of Palm Beach.

57 In some places, the Oceanic coastline rises up to form steep, jagged cliffs which are the ideal training ground for rock and free climbers.

58-59 Every year since 1945, the most famous regatta in the world has started from Sydney Harbour. This "Blue Water Classic", better known as the "Sydney-Hobart", is run over a distance of 680 sea miles.

60 Some children playing among the waves of Palm Beach, one of Sydney's most exclusive residential quarters, home to industrial magnates and film producers.

61 Bondi Beach is not only a splendid beach for relaxation and sunbathing but also a necessary decompression chamber for the populous eastern suburbs.

62-63 Wind-surfing is becoming constantly more popular among young people and Sydney's beaches are the setting for dozens of international competitions every year.

When you once more have your feet on dry land, at Circular Quay, you will be welcomed by a mixture of office workers and tourists enjoying the sun. Sydney has a temperate climate and this is reflected in the character of its inhabitants. The original Anglo-Saxon monopoly has been greatly diluted since the Second World War following massive immigration from Europe, South East Asia, China and the Islands of the Pacific. The result is a multiracial mix, unique in Australia, which is reflected above all in the appearance of the city, whose charm derives from the juxtaposition of the different styles which have succeeded each other in the course of the years. Bricks and concrete, wrought-iron and plastic: Victorian, Art Nouveau and modern styles stand next to each other without any embarrassment.

Fortunately in the midst of the skyscrapers there are numerous strategically placed cafés with sidewalk tables and terraces, pedestrian zones, tranquil parks and public gardens, ideal for moments of relaxation.

For those who want to do a bit of shopping, it is useful to bear in mind that the large department stores in the city sell a selection of goods similar to those to be found in Europe. The shopping arcade is decidedly more Australian. One shopping mall is a real architectural monument dating from the beginning of this century: the "Strand" in George Street.

The nearby Martin Place is a spacious pedestrian street which divides an area of offices in the north from that of shops and entertainment in the south. Dixon Street is the heart of Chinatown with its rich proliferation of restaurants and shops in oriental style.

If it is true that in the luxurious residential quarter of Double Bay, the wealthy Knox Street is the "Mayfair" of Sydney, it is equally true that enormous shopping centres dominate the suburbs; for example, the one at Birkenhead Point even contains a museum of the sea.

On Saturday mornings you can go for a stroll around Sydney's biggest market, "Paddy's Market" or else loaf about in the flea markets of Paddington or the traditional working-class suburb of Balmain or visit one of the famous Sydney bars where the glasses of beer change name according to their size. The state of New South Wales has licensing laws which are the most liberal in the entire nation and the clients of the bars are always numerous.

The most characteristic bars, tiled with white majolica, are to be found in the port of the Rocks: The "Hero of Waterloo" and the "Lord Nelson" are the oldest.

64 The "surf culture" has become part of the lifestyle and language of thousands of Australians, sustaining an industry which declares a turnover of many tens of millions of dollars a year.

65 A water-scooter in the waters of Manly. Any excuse is good for tackling the waves of the Pacific on the most varied means of transport.

66 Despite the fashions, surfing continues to be the aquatic sport par excellence and this might be due to the fact that, as inveterate surfers like to recall: "the waves are free". Every year specialized industries turn out something like 45,000 surfboards and over half a million various accessories.

67 The passion for the waves is so much alive that even on dry land the young Sydney-siders feel the need to recreate the emotions of surfing by carrying out reckless manoeuvres on their skateboards.

68 Every beach on the ocean has its Surf Lifesaving Club whose members, all volunteers, patrol the coast to prevent all types of accident. In more than 80 years of activity, these associations has saved more than 20,000 human lives.

69 There are numerous female lifesavers and among their tasks is that of indicating the safety of each beach with flags.

70-71 In the course of the popular summer meetings known as Surf Carnivals, the members of the city's 24 lifesaving clubs challenge each other to races in the waves of the Pacific on board heavy rowing boats normally used for rescuing people at sea.

72-73 They say that in Sydney there is the right sport for everyone and despite its antiquated and rather working-class image, bowls has a large following and there are many extremely exclusive greens and clubs.

74 *A jet of the Australian airline, Qantas, flies over the suburban quarter of Pyrmont. In the foreground is a merchant ship moored at the Glebe Island terminal in Darling Harbour.*

75 *The old brick houses in Lower Fort Street, now a protected monument, recall what Sydney must have looked like in the last century before its rapid growth.*

76 Sydney's old Astronomical Observatory stands isolated on the highest natural site in the city – the summit of Observatory Hill in the Rocks. The telescopes were used from 1858 to 1982 when the complex was turned into a museum. Today the large but antiquated optic systems can be used on request by amateur astronomers.

77 Taronga Park in Mosman Bay is considered one of the most beautiful zoological gardens in the world and among its more than 5,000 animals there are, obviously, exclusively Australian species such as platypuses, emus, kangaroos, koalas and echidnas.

78 After a complete restoration costing more than 75 million dollars, the elegant balconied galleries of the Queen Victoria Building have returned to their former splendour, thanks to the skilful juxtaposition of Victorian architecture with a modern service structure.

79 The typically Australian "shopping arcades", especially the most famous ones in Sydney, contain not only elegant commercial areas but also crowded meeting places and glittering shop windows which give an insight into the taste and style of the city.

80 The stretch of George Street which intersects with the Rocks district still maintains intact the 18th-century appearance of the buildings. Rocks is the "cradle of the nation", the birthplace of Sydney, and has known a long period of decline and neglect; fortunately starting in the 1960s a grand restoration plan gave back charm and dignity to depots, warehouses and barracks which are now used as shops and art galleries.

81 George Street, the High Street of Governor Phillip's day, was given its present name in honour of King George III. The flyover which crosses the road is the Cahill Expressway, one of the approach roads to the Harbour Bridge.

Sydney-siders know how to enjoy themselves and at night theatres, restaurants and discothèques transform themselves into melting pots full of the most interesting types of people. Around 60 clubs present live musical groups catering for all tastes.

For the more traditionally-minded, there are several theatres where one can choose between dramatic authors, musical comedies and good avant-garde entertainment. If, on the other hand, you want to have a more intense experience, remember that if London has Soho, Paris has Pigalle and Tokyo has Ginza, it is also true that Sydney has King's Cross, the only environment of this type in the whole of Australia. "The Cross" is the most densely populated square mile of the entire city in which there are an incredible number of pizzerias and ethnic restaurants, night clubs, sex-shops and rather eccentric meeting places. Darlinghurst Road is the temple of consumerism – a large electric circus open all night for insomniacs who prefer strong-tasting urban adventures. In the centre of this mad confusion is the circular fountain of the El Alamein Memorial, while no more than 300 feet from Fitzroy Gardens is the Wayside Chapel, a church that is possibly unique in that it has the peculiarity of not professing any particular credo. Open to all religions, it sets out to be an oasis of peace and a spiritual refuge from the stress and the temptations of the modern metropolis.

If you are impressed by so much originality and you like unusual places, you ought to pass a Sunday afternoon in the Domain, a famous city park where amusement is guaranteed. The absolute freedom of speech is the stimulus which makes a phenomenal assortment of strange people, idealists and radicals, climb onto their empty soap boxes and harangue the crowd with speeches and all sorts of arguments ranging from politics and the growing of begonias to the infringed rights of the Aborigines and youth problems.

The Domain and the Botanical Gardens form a vast area of well-kept lawns and exotic flowers perfect for strolling or relaxation; exhibitions of figurative art are often organized in the park. At the weekend crowds of people visit these metropolitan oases, which are a pleasant change for those who work all week in the business district. Here, you can meet entire families of Greeks eating traditional food, old couples and young lovers, ecologists and sun-worshipers, practitioners of martial arts and several hundred thoroughly absorbed chess-players. The inhabitants of Sydney love to be in the midst of greenery and you can easily confirm this fact by walking around Observatory Hill, the highest point of the city, or central Hyde Park in which there are three large fountains. Centennial Park is the most extensive public garden in the city with a surface area of 540 acres: its nine lakes attract different species of aquatic birds in each season. It is even possible to hire a horse or a bicycle and ride through the park and there are also well equipped keep-fit paths for fitness freaks.

Some Sydney-siders are enthusiasts for physical activity and right from the very early morning determined joggers run past those few others who, heedless of them, prefer to have a quiet stroll or sunbathe on the lawns (it is not forbidden to tread on

them). The students, in particular, dedicate themselves to sport and there are a lot of students in Sydney. The University was founded in 1852 and is the oldest in the entire continent.
As in the rest of the country the sports which are the most keenly followed are tennis, golf and cricket, but the specialities of Sydney are surf, regattas and Rugby League which is played by 15 teams representing the different city districts and country areas.
If all this movement should make you shudder and you are more inclined to study fine arts and history, Sydney is pleased to satisfy your desires in this field, too. The Australian Museum is dedicated to Natural History and the large deserts as well as to Aboriginal and Melanesian art; the Art Gallery of New South Wales boasts an exhaustive collection of European painting from the Renaissance to Picasso as well as the work of 19th- and 20th-century Australian and Aboriginal artists.

82 top The Australian Museum houses collections of natural history, Aboriginal and Melanesian art and a gallery specifically dedicated to the geology of Australia.

82 bottom A very rich collection of works by European artists dating from the Renaissance to modern times as well as works by Australian artists are on show in the rooms of the Art Gallery of New South Wales.

83 The monument outside the Art Gallery of New South Wales shows the effects of the stylistic teachings of Classicism.

84 A hydrofoil of the Urban Transit Authority entering the waters of the Harbour. The passenger service between the city and the outlying suburbs has become extremely comfortable and rapid following the introduction of these nimble and speedy vessels.

85 On both sides of Bridge Street in the pulsating heart of the city there are orderly lines of luxury international hotels, banks and government offices.

86-87 A persistent veil of morning mist transfigures the outline of the Opera House, making it look like a mythological creature.

88 The panorama is particularly gentle and evocative in the first hours of dawn when the first rays of the sun are reflected in the colossal prisms of the skyscrapers.

89 A dreamlike image of Harbour Bridge shrouded in morning mist.

Sydney is not possessive and willingly gives everyone the right to feel at home, as if he had lived there all his life. Moreover, once arrived, the visitor soon realizes that the range of things to do is enormous.

For the more adventurous, a visit to the city can turn into an exploration for which the voluminous Gregory's city map, which even the Sydney-siders admit to needing, is indispensable.

For the more dynamic types, we would suggest renting a boat and sailing in the magnificent waters that make up Sydney Harbour. In the midst of hundreds of vessels manoeuvering about in the bay there is only one rule which must be respected scrupulously: the hovercrafts, which operate a passenger service towards Manly beach, have right of way over all other boats, including yours.

For the more reflective spirits, it is perhaps worth recalling the popular saying which claims that there is nothing more typically Australian than lying on a long, soft, white stretch of sand and relaxing completely.

To the visitor and the inhabitant of the 1990s, Sydney offers a unique and exciting mix of interesting things, including several wildlife reserves for rare animals within 20 miles of the city.

If you are patient and lucky you might see some koala bears, kangaroos, wombats and dingos. Sydney has something to offer everyone, whatever their interest.

90 A young bride and bridegroom have their photograph taken on the steps of the Opera House.

91 The City, observed at dusk from the calm tranquillity of Circular Quay, takes on a particular charm, almost as if the city wanted to disassociate itself from the frenzied rhythms of the day and to find a moment of reflection.

92 The steel arch of the Harbour Bridge reaches a height of 436 feet but during the summer, the heat makes it expand, adding another seven inches to its overall height.

93 Compared with the immense extent of the built-up area of Greater Sydney, the heart of the city is relatively compact.

94-95 The metal structures of Harbour Bridge reveal their massive complexity when lit at night, against the backdrop of the city.